T0031712

BAREFOOT BOOKS

WATER

A Deep Dive of Discovery

WRITTEN BY **Christy Mihaly**

ILLUSTRATED BY **Mariona Cabassa**

Barefoot Books
Step inside a story

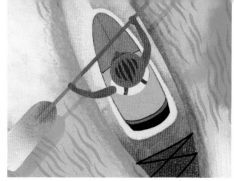

CONTENTS

This magnifying glass invites you to take a closer look at the science of water. Special boxes throughout the book bring the science into focus.

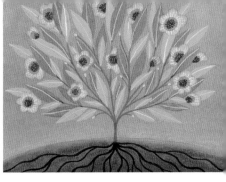

Welcome to the world of water!

DIVE DEEPER!

Watch for special boxes like this!

Here you'll find ideas for:

- **ACTIVITIES** to learn more
- **EXPERIMENTS** to do at home
- **ACTIONS** to help protect water

Raindrops Fall Around the Globe

Plip! Plop! Plitter! Plosh!

Raindrops fall from the clouds

onto rooftops and umbrellas, cars and gardens.

What happens to the rain? Where does the water go?

Follow me, I'll show you!

SPLASH!
Onto a roof,
down to the pavement,
across the road.

SWIRL!
Other drops join in
and we flow along,
collecting dirt, oil,
maybe an insect or two.

SWOOSH!
We stream faster and wider,
down the hill into brooks and rivers,
onwards towards the sea . . .

4

Raindrops fall around the world
onto cities and forests and fields.
They sink into soil and plop into puddles.

Eventually, in a day or a month or over many years, the water will find
its way to the ocean. Earth's ocean covers most of the planet's surface.
The oceans are so vast that when astronauts look down from space,
Earth looks mostly blue.

But Earth's water doesn't just sit there.
It's in motion, even within the ocean.

I travel all around the ocean, from the
Arctic to Antarctica — and back!
Come on, let's explore the world of water!

Our WATERY World

We usually think of Earth as, well, earth . . . meaning dirt or dry ground. But Earth is mostly water!

How much water? Enough to cover **71%** of the globe. Scientists estimate that all the water on Earth adds up to about 326 million trillion gallons.

That's this much:

326,000,000,000,000,000,000 gallons
(1,234,000,000,000,000,000,000 L).

DIVE DEEPER!

How much water do you use?

6

All of Earth's water is important.
But only a small part of it is drinkable.
The ocean is too salty —
        our bodies can't handle it.

Less than 1% of the water on Earth is good for drinking!

Of all Earth's water:

97% is in the OCEAN

whose wide waters stretch from waves breaking on beaches to the vast open seas, from mysterious deep, dark depths to sparkling blue, coral-filled **lagoons**.

2% is frozen as **ICE** including at the North Pole, on Antarctica and in **glaciers**.

1% is **FRESH WATER**

including lakes, rivers and streams. Some people call this "sweet water." It doesn't contain the dissolved salts that the ocean does. Most of the world's fresh water isn't on the surface, though! You'll find it here:

- 💧 under the ground (**groundwater**)
- 💧 in the dirt (soil moisture)
- 💧 in the air (water vapor)

7

Tekelmarae and the Boy Who Remembered

VANUATU

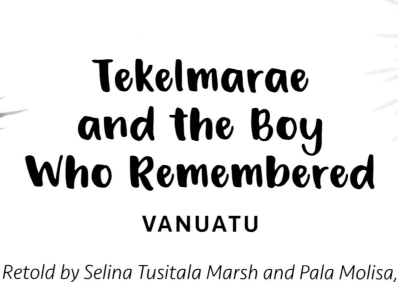

Retold by Selina Tusitala Marsh and Pala Molisa,
as told by Ripae Mandei Tutuhun

Tekelmarae, the Eel River Guardian of Fun and Love, protects the blue waters of Vanlav, where people gather to fish and play. The people dance in fun, swim in love and every year give thanks for all the good things that come from the mountain — especially the fish.

It is custom that you use all of someone's names when you thank them properly. Names hold stories. Stories hold the magic of a people. Tekelmarae has three names. Every year, the people gathered to chant:

Your first name is Tekelmarae – Your second name is fun
Your third name is love – We name you for everyone.

They watched Tekelmarae dart out from his hole like a flash of black lightning. They *oohed* and *aahed* at his long, black body and waited for his reply:

The river flows – From mountain to sea – I am the river – The river is me.

The river then giggled with silvery fish.

But over time, the people began to forget the River Guardian's names. One year, the people were so busy working in town, they forgot the third name. Tekelmarae only came out to his white, milky belly. The next year, the people were so busy at church, they forgot the second name. Tekelmarae only poked out his black, inky head.

The following year, the people were so busy cutting trees on the plantation, they forgot the first name. Now all the names had been forgotten! Tekelmarae was nowhere to be seen.

"River Guardian! Come out! The water is low. The fish are dying!" the people cried. From inside the hole, they heard a whisper:

People of Vanlav - You have forgotten Fun and Love
The river will not flow - From mountain to sea
You have forgotten my names - You have forgotten me.

Silence. Everyone thought that Tekelmarae was dead. They left to go back to work. But Majijiki, the littlest boy, lingered. He began crying:

River Guardian - Can't you see? - You are the river - And the river is me.

The water flickered. Majijiki cried again:

River Eel - Hear my plea - Tell me your names - So we can all be free.

The water exploded with a flash of black lightning.

I am Tekelmarae - I am the same - Feel me, feel me - What is my name?

Majijiki put one hand into the water and felt the eel's heart beating slower. Was the eel dying? He couldn't lose his beloved eel! As the eel slipped slowly out of his hands, the tail flicked his palm. Majijiki giggled. He softly poked the eel's belly, teasing, "Tickle, tickle."

"Nearly," the eel replied.

"Tickle? Tekel! Tekel . . . marae!" Majijiki laughed out loud. Then the boy remembered.

Your first name is Tekelmarae - Your second name is Fun
Your third name is Love - I name you for everyone.

Tekelmarae swished his tail in the rising waters, now full of laughing fish:

People of Fun and Love - To always be free
Know you are the river - Know you are me.

Map of Marvels

Amazon River, South America

Ⓐ Longest river:

The Nile or the Amazon? You'd think it would be easy to tell which is longer, but not everyone agrees exactly where these rivers begin and end. Not only that, varying rainfall can make a river shift its path over time, changing its overall length. For many years, Africa's Nile has been considered the longest. It winds about 4,160 miles (6,695 km) through parts of ten countries in Africa and into the Mediterranean Sea in Egypt. But some scientists think the Amazon River is longer. The Amazon travels at least 4,000 miles (6,440 km) across South America from Peru to Brazil, emptying into the Atlantic Ocean.

Nile River, Africa

Ⓑ Tallest waterfall:

At Angel Falls in Venezuela, the water crashes down 3,212 feet (979 m) from the top to bottom. That's as tall as 178 giraffes!

PAGE 20
The Waters of Sulis ENGLAND

NORTH AMERICA

Travel to page 51 to meet **AUTUMN PELTIER**, a clean water activist in Canada.

ATLANTIC OCEAN

SOUTH AMERICA

Dip into page 47 to see how **GEORGIE BADIEL** of Burkina Faso uses water to help girls go to school.

...p page 39 to ...wonders that ...brings to the ...N Rainforest.

SOUTHERN OCEAN

ARCTIC OCEAN

EUROPE

D

C

A

AFRICA

INDIAN OCEAN

Visit page 38 to read
about the great **SAHARA**,
where water is scarce.

ANTARCTICA

OUR ENORMOUS OCEAN

You might have heard of the five oceans: the Atlantic, Pacific, Arctic, Indian and Southern Oceans. But these are not really five separate oceans. They are all connected, as you can see on this map. People have given different areas of the ocean these separate names, but they all are actually a part of one very big ocean.

The ocean is full of life: It's home to Earth's very largest and very smallest animals. The ocean also causes changes to the **weather** on land. Much of our rain comes from rainstorms that form at sea. The ocean influences our temperatures too. When sunlight hits the ocean, the water absorbs heat from the sun. Ocean waters move that warmth around the globe.

Over the years, the ocean has been getting warmer and that has been changing the planet's **climate**. Climate means the usual weather patterns over a long period of time. As average temperatures of both the air and the ocean rise, scientists study the ocean for clues about the future of Earth's climate.

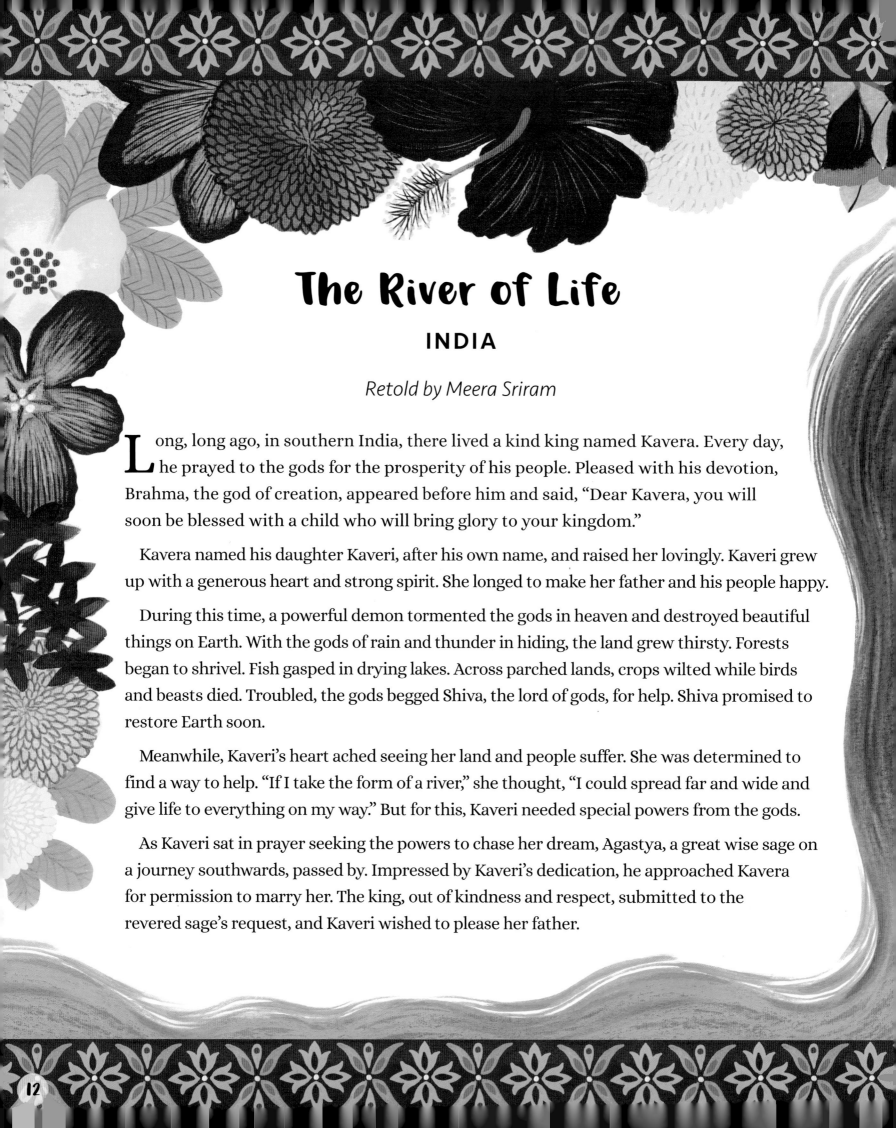

The River of Life

INDIA

Retold by Meera Sriram

Long, long ago, in southern India, there lived a kind king named Kavera. Every day, he prayed to the gods for the prosperity of his people. Pleased with his devotion, Brahma, the god of creation, appeared before him and said, "Dear Kavera, you will soon be blessed with a child who will bring glory to your kingdom."

Kavera named his daughter Kaveri, after his own name, and raised her lovingly. Kaveri grew up with a generous heart and strong spirit. She longed to make her father and his people happy.

During this time, a powerful demon tormented the gods in heaven and destroyed beautiful things on Earth. With the gods of rain and thunder in hiding, the land grew thirsty. Forests began to shrivel. Fish gasped in drying lakes. Across parched lands, crops wilted while birds and beasts died. Troubled, the gods begged Shiva, the lord of gods, for help. Shiva promised to restore Earth soon.

Meanwhile, Kaveri's heart ached seeing her land and people suffer. She was determined to find a way to help. "If I take the form of a river," she thought, "I could spread far and wide and give life to everything on my way." But for this, Kaveri needed special powers from the gods.

As Kaveri sat in prayer seeking the powers to chase her dream, Agastya, a great wise sage on a journey southwards, passed by. Impressed by Kaveri's dedication, he approached Kavera for permission to marry her. The king, out of kindness and respect, submitted to the revered sage's request, and Kaveri wished to please her father.

However, Kaveri's mind was still set on her desire to water the land. She was going to keep her dream alive. Finally, she spoke up, "I will marry Agastya on one condition. He can never leave me alone. Not even for a moment. And if he does, I will forsake him to follow my heart and serve the people." The sage agreed and they married.

One day, Agastya wanted to set out to meditate on a faraway hilltop. Afraid to leave Kaveri alone, he used his yogic powers and transformed her into water, so he could carry her with him in his small waterpot. Restless, Kaveri sloshed inside, waiting for her chance.

As Agastya sat with eyes closed, Shiva, who had also been waiting for the right moment to save the land, watched from above. He sent his son, Ganesha, to release Kaveri. Ganesha morphed into a crow, swooped down the hill, and knocked the waterpot over. Kaveri eagerly spilled onto the cracked earth, her dream finally flowing into the world.

Agastya was enraged. But the crow briefly revealed his true self as he flapped away. And the sage soon realized it was the work of Shiva.

It was time for Kaveri to rise.

Kaveri bubbled into a small pool and gurgled as she scampered across rocks and crooks. She quenched the dry earth and brought it to life again. As she meandered through valleys and plains, flowers bloomed and fields flourished.

Kaveri swelled into a mighty river and snaked through lands before merging into the deep sea. Along the serene banks of the Kaveri River, the kingdom thrived. Poets sang her glory and scholars praised her bounty.

Kaveri was born to give life. And as a river, she did just that.

WATER the Shape-Shifter

Water is ordinary, everyday stuff.
But water is also extraordinary and powerful.
Water can change its shape.

A mountain lake's cool blue water — **LIQUID** —
transforms into slippery white ice — **SOLID** —
or rises into the air as an invisible vapor — **GAS**.

LIQUID: Going with the Flow

As a droplet, I'm a liquid! But I can also change into a solid or a gas.

You see water all around you,
in ponds and puddles and pipes.
You drink it and use it to wash and cook.
Water trickles and ripples,
it flows and it floods.
It fills the oceans.
Water also hides beneath our feet.

Rainwater drops to the dirt and sinks in. It collects as groundwater beneath the surface. This water is stored between little bits of soil and sand, within cracked and broken rocks, under layers of earth. There's more water underground than in all of Earth's lakes and rivers.

Groundwater may stay hidden for thousands of years or it may quickly return to the surface, bubbling up in springs or rejoining rivers. Groundwater can also be pumped up to the surface. Even in the **desert**, people drill wells deep into the earth to reach a supply of underground water — water for drinking, washing, watering crops and more.

ATOMS & MOLECULES

Water gets special powers from its basic structure — its **atoms** and molecules.

Atoms are so tiny you can't see them, even with a regular microscope. They are the basic building blocks of all physical stuff, or **matter**. Everything from this book to a distant planet to a drop of blood is made of atoms.

There are 118 known different types of atoms on Earth, known as **elements**. Examples of elements include lead, gold, hydrogen and **oxygen**.

Atoms combine to make molecules, which are still much too small to see. To make a molecule of water requires 3 atoms: 2 hydrogen (H) plus 1 oxygen (O). That's why the scientific symbol for water is H_2O.

Why is water so good at dissolving things like salt? The answer lies in the molecules. A water molecule is like a magnet in that one part (the hydrogen) has a positive charge and the other part (the oxygen) has a negative charge. Molecules of table salt (sodium chloride) are made of sodium (Na) and chlorine (Cl) atoms. The sodium has a positive (+) charge. The chlorine has a negative (-) charge, which makes it chloride.

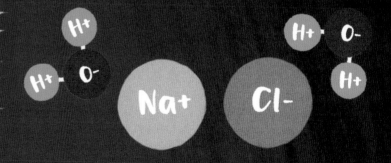

When water molecules meet salt molecules, the oxygen side of the water molecules attracts the sodium while the hydrogen side attracts the chloride. They pull strongly enough to break the salt molecules apart.

Here's more water magic!

Water dissolves some things. When you add salt to water, you can see it mix in, disappearing into the liquid. Water can dissolve more materials than any other liquid.

What makes this happen? **Molecules**!

The water in the ocean contains dissolved salt . . . it tastes salty!

DIVE DEEPER!

What dissolves in water?

Sometimes harmful materials dissolve in water, making it polluted — dirty and not good to drink. But nature has some solutions to this **pollution**. When dirty water flows through sand or certain rocks, or swamps and marshes, the pollutants can be trapped, making the water cleaner.

SOLID: FROSTY FREEZE

When water gets cold enough to freeze,
it turns into ice. Ice for skating!
Tiny ice crystals that fall as snowflakes!
Snow for snowmen and skiing!

You might find ice in frosty cubes in your freezer,
as a sneaky, slippery coating on a cold pavement,
or clinging in delicate, dangly icicles
along the edge of a roof in winter.

DIVE DEEPER!

What can melt ice?

SLOW MOLECULES AHEAD

Water molecules are in constant motion. Water
changes its form depending on how fast its molecules
are moving. When temperatures get colder, water
molecules move more slowly. At 32°F (0°C), they slow
down enough to stick together and form a solid — ice.

Most liquids shrink when they freeze. Not water — it expands!
When water freezes, its molecules join together in a solid network,
or lattice. Within this lattice, the molecules are further apart than
when they are moving separately in cold liquid water. They take up
more space in their solid form. That's why ice floats!

Now I'm frozen!

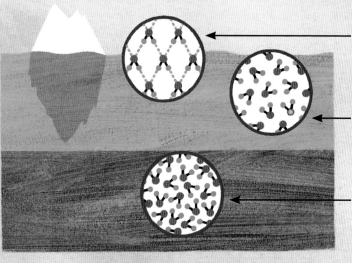

ICE (molecules locked
in place with air
trapped in between)

WARMER WATER
(molecules move
faster, further apart)

COLDER WATER
(molecules move
slowly, closer together)

In cold places all around the Earth, you'll find massive, mountainous mounds of ice called glaciers. Glaciers form over many years, as piles of snow press down and turn icy. They sit high on cold mountaintops from Alaska to Africa to the Andes — on every continent except Australia.

Glacier ice takes on different shapes.

At the North Pole, big sheets of ice float atop the Arctic Ocean. Around the South Pole, the continent of Antarctica is covered with the largest expanse of ice on the planet. The vast Antarctic Ice Sheet (see map on pages 10–11) is as big as the United States and Mexico combined.

Glaciers and patches of ice hold buried treasures. Things that have been frozen in ice for thousands of years don't decay, or rot. As Earth's ancient ice melts, it reveals long-frozen surprises.

In the mountains of Norway, along the edges of melting glaciers, scientists have found ancient objects. They were left by the Vikings, the Norse warriors who lived there a thousand years ago. Clothing and wooden skis, which would have rotted at warmer temperatures, are in great shape after their centuries-long deep freeze.

In northern Russia, people have discovered whole woolly mammoths frozen in the ice. Woolly mammoths died out about 10,000 years ago!

One fine day in 1991, two hikers in the mountains between Italy and Austria stumbled across a human body in the ice. The ice had kept the body, now known as Ötzi the Iceman, in good condition for more than 5,000 years.

GAS: Vanishing into the Air

Just as you need water to drink, you need oxygen to breathe.
Oxygen is a **gas** — one of many gases in the air.
Gases are all around us, though we usually can't see or feel them.
The air we breathe is made mostly of a gas called nitrogen.
What's another gas in our air?
Water vapor.

Molecules in Motion

While water turns to ice when it cools, it turns to gas when it heats up. How does water turn into gas?

When water molecules get hot, they move faster. When they jiggle really fast, they break out of the liquid and rise into the air as a gas. That's **evaporation**. You can see evaporation at work — if you leave a wet towel out in the sun, it dries. The water rises from the towel into the air.

Sometimes, ice turns directly into water vapor, without first becoming water. This happens in snowy mountains when hot, dry winds blow across the icy peaks. That's called **sublimation**.

The opposite of sublimation is **deposition**, when water turns directly from a gas to a solid. When the ground is very cold, water comes out of the air and leaves a sparkly blanket of ice crystals — frost — on the ground.

DIVE DEEPER!

Where did the water go?

18

Water evaporates, or rises into the air, from the ocean, lakes, ponds and puddles. It can evaporate out of your water glass. And it can also come from you!

If you wear a face mask or scarf wrapped around your nose and mouth, you might notice it gets damp when you breathe. That's because your breath contains water vapor.

Plants, too, send water vapor into the air. Water moves from the soil through the roots up a plant's stem to its leaves and evaporates there.

Water vapor is invisible.

But, sometimes . . .
When white steam rises from your kettle,
when clouds form high in the sky,
or when warm, moist air meets cool, dry air
and a misty fog appears, what's happening?
That's **condensation**!
When you breathe out on a chilly day and
your warm breath hits the cold air, that's
condensation too: The water is changing
from its gas form to liquid form.
What you're seeing then is tiny liquid
water droplets in the air.

Now you see me, now you don't!

The Waters of Sulis

ENGLAND

Retold by Xanthe Gresham Knight

There was once a boy called Bladud, but everyone called him Wolf. He was strong — so strong that even his hair curled like snakes, like flames. One breakfast, his mother, the Queen, said, "I dreamed the river spoke, 'Wolf must give his strength to Sulis.'"

"Who — and what — is Sulis?" asked Wolf.

"A goddess of fire and water," replied his mother.

"Scary!"

She smiled. "You, scared? You who can overtake the wind? Are you afraid of the sun on your face? The streams you bathe in?"

Wolf went down to the water. "How can I give Sulis my strength?" he asked his reflection. Sunlight blurred his eyes so that rivulets turned to rainbows, and rainbows to a dancing goddess. "Sulis?" Wolf dived in and swam fast, giving his strength to the river. "There!" He panted, clambering up the bank. Flattening some mud, Wolf carved Sulis's image — his own face with water spirals for hair. Once it was dry, he strung it round his neck.

Wolf and his mother loved to imitate other animals, barking like pups, honking like geese. While they were tumbling, she touched a lump on his arm. Wolf yelped. The Queen found sores all over him. She knew he must have leprosy.

She applied herbs and prayed, "Don't let him die! Take me instead." His mother's prayer was answered. Her last words were, "Remember what the river said? You must give your strength to Sulis. Look after her and she'll look after you."

Wolf's heart was so full of pain, he wondered how it fit inside his body. When the King locked him up to stop his disease spreading, Wolf escaped through a chimney. He had to get to the river.

Alone, hair falling, sores multiplying, Wolf followed a drift of pigs beside the water, imitating their grunts as if playing with his mother. Like him, they had a skin disease. Shaking with fever, he collapsed under an oak as the pigs wallowed in a misty swamp. Days later, Wolf woke dreaming his mother was covering his body with fistfuls of hot sludge. The pigs were snuffling close. He noticed their sores had healed. "Mud!"

Wolf waded in. "So warm!" He stretched and *Snap!* his pendant sank into the ooze. "Sulis!" he cried. In reply, a bubbling at his feet, a rushing at his back. Wolf pulled stones and sticks from a gap in the rock behind him and hot water gushed, creating a green pool. Wolf floated, letting the water hold him. As the days passed, Sulis's strength entered his bones, taking the aching. "Thank you." Wolf murmured.

Hair thick, skin smooth, Wolf raised dripping arms towards the sun. "My strength is your strength!" he called to Sulis.

In gratitude, Wolf used all his energy to build the city of Bath around the life-giving pool. Word spread. From town to city, city to continent, people flocked to be healed.

And they still come to Bath to be cured by the waters of Sulis. Scientists say it's not a goddess, but minerals — sulphate, calcium and chloride — that work the magic. Even so, the sign of Bath is still Wolf's face, framed by the hair of Sulis, which curls like snakes, like flames.

Recycled WATER

Water's shape-shifting power helps it circle around the Earth in a dance called the **water cycle**.

Would you believe I'm billions of years old?

THE WATER CYCLE

The water cycle is powered by energy from the sun. The sun's rays beat down on the water below. When the sun warms the water enough, it causes **EVAPORATION**. That's when liquid water becomes a gas, rising into the air. As water vapor, it joins the blanket of gases around Earth — the atmosphere.

Water doesn't stay in the air for long. It loses its heat. Through **CONDENSATION**, the gas turns back into liquid water droplets. Water droplets stick to tiny bits of dust floating in the air. When enough of these come together, they form clouds.

More droplets join the cloud, and they become larger and heavier. When they get heavy enough, they fall to Earth. That's called **PRECIPITATION**. If it's not too cold, the water falls to Earth as rain. Air temperatures below freezing (32°F / 0°C) result in frozen precipitation such as snow or sleet.

Water flows from streams and rivers into ponds, lakes and oceans. This is called **COLLECTION**. Some water sinks into the soil and collects underground. In very cold places, water freezes into solid ice and may remain frozen for hundreds, thousands or even hundreds of thousands of years. Eventually, warmed by the sun, it melts. As the sun shines on, water warms and evaporates and its journey continues.

CONDENSATION

PRECIPITATION

EVAPORATION

COLLECTION

DRINKING THE SAME OLD WATER?

You might notice something interesting about the water cycle: It's the same water, going around and around and around. The water cycle cannot create new water.

How long has this been going on? For about four billion years. That's how old Earth's water is.

You know what that means? You could be drinking the very same water that a dinosaur once drank.

But . . . wouldn't four-billion-year-old water get kind of dirty? Relax! The water cycle helps clean the water so it's good to use over and over and over. (Look under the flap!)

DIVE DEEPER!

How can you help keep Earth's water clean?

Here are some ideas:

- In your garden, use natural products that won't pollute groundwater.

- Recycle your batteries or use rechargeable ones. Some batteries contain poisonous chemicals that can leak from landfills and get into our water.

- In your home, use natural cleaners such as vinegar and lemons, so you don't send harsh or toxic chemicals down the drain.

THE GOLDILOCKS ZONE

Earth's temperature range makes the water cycle possible. If Earth were too hot or too cold, our water would always be gas or ice. That's why scientists say Earth is in the Goldilocks Zone — just right for liquid water to exist, which all living things need to survive.

TOO HOT   **JUST RIGHT**   **TOO COLD**

WATER is Life

Everybody's thirsty!
Birds and butterflies need water.
Bears, belugas, bats, beagles and bacteria.
Plants need water too:
Bamboo, birch trees, broccoli plants,
banana trees, begonias and buttercups.
All living things on Earth need water.

ANIMALS: Sip, Swallow, Swig

All animals — including people —
need water for their bodies and brains to work properly.

Water helps you keep your cool. When you sweat, water leaves
your body through tiny openings, called pores, in your skin.
When that water evaporates into the air, it also takes heat
away from your body.

Water also cushions your joints — like knees and ankles —
and helps them move more smoothly. And water helps
your body break down food and brings the
nutrients to where your body needs them.
Finally, water carries your
body's waste away.

How much water is in your body?

- When you were born, you were about 75% water.
- By the age of one, you were about 65% water.
- An average adult's body is about 60% water.
- An elderly person's body is only about 50% water.

You can see that as you get older, you get a little drier. As a baby grows and starts to eat food, the makeup of its body changes. Over time, the body's water content goes down. That's because of things like how your kidneys work, how much you sweat and how your body processes food and water.

Where is all this water in your body? Different parts contain different amounts of water. Blood plasma (the liquid part of your blood) is about 90% water.

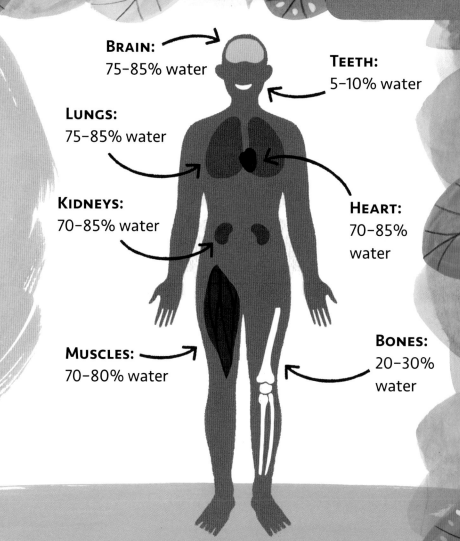

BRAIN: 75–85% water

TEETH: 5–10% water

LUNGS: 75–85% water

KIDNEYS: 70–85% water

HEART: 70–85% water

MUSCLES: 70–80% water

BONES: 20–30% water

Drink up! It's good for your health.

How much water does your body need?

The amount of water you need each day depends on your size, how much you're exercising, how hot the weather is and all sorts of other factors. You can get the water your body needs by drinking it, of course. You also take in water from other drinks, and from the food you eat, especially fruits and vegetables. These guidelines show the total amount of water you should get each day.

- **4 TO 8 YEARS OLD:** about 7 cups of water. A couple of cups will come from your food, so try to drink about 5 cups of water (and other drinks).

- **9 TO 13 YEARS OLD:** about 9 to 10 cups of water. A couple of cups will come from your food, so try to drink about 7 to 8 cups of water (and other drinks).

PLANTS: Roots to Shoots

Plants are thirsty too. Like animals, they are made up mostly of water. Water helps keep the plants' stems and leaves firm and healthy. It also helps plants grow and make seeds.

The majestic redwood trees that grow along the coast of northern California and southern Oregon in North America are the world's tallest trees (see map on pages 10–11). They carry water from the soil up, up, up, to the treetops, as high as 350 feet (107 m). That's taller than the Statue of Liberty!

Plants "sweat" too — most of the water they take up through their roots goes back into the air through tiny holes in their leaves. This keeps the plants cool. When plants release water like this, it's called **transpiration**.

But plants also use water to do something animals can't: They make their own food. That's right! Plants make food using water, air and sunlight. They do this through a process called **photosynthesis**.

How does photosynthesis happen? Plants draw water from the soil through their roots and into their stems and leaves. In addition, through tiny holes in their leaves and stems, plants absorb the gas **carbon dioxide** from the air. When sunlight hits a plant's leaves, it provides energy that allows the plant to transform the water and carbon dioxide into its own food — a sugar called glucose!

Plants need glucose in order to grow — to build stems and roots and leaves and fruits. And the sugar in those plant parts is also food for animals (and people) that eat them.

Photosynthesis has another bonus, too: It produces oxygen that animals need to breathe. Thank goodness for water and sunshine and plants!

Without water, plants will wilt!

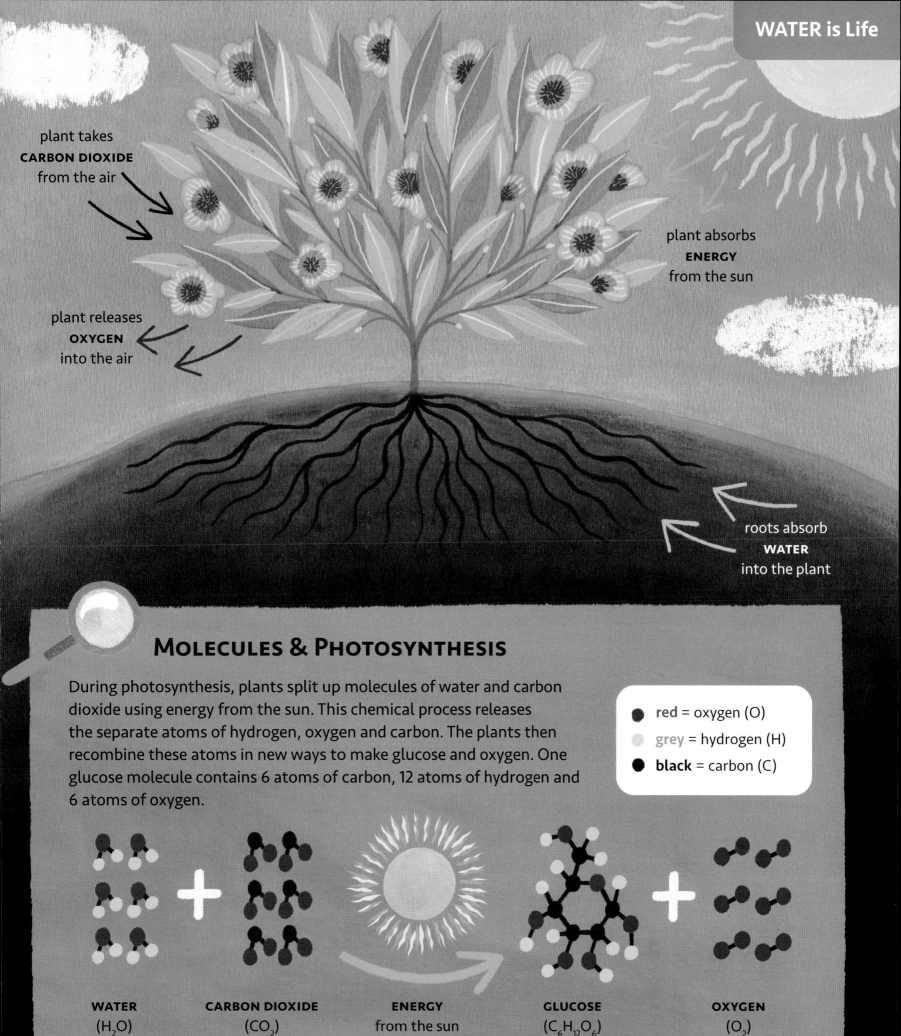

plant takes
CARBON DIOXIDE
from the air

plant absorbs
ENERGY
from the sun

plant releases
OXYGEN
into the air

roots absorb
WATER
into the plant

MOLECULES & PHOTOSYNTHESIS

During photosynthesis, plants split up molecules of water and carbon dioxide using energy from the sun. This chemical process releases the separate atoms of hydrogen, oxygen and carbon. The plants then recombine these atoms in new ways to make glucose and oxygen. One glucose molecule contains 6 atoms of carbon, 12 atoms of hydrogen and 6 atoms of oxygen.

● **red** = oxygen (O)
● **grey** = hydrogen (H)
● **black** = carbon (C)

WATER
(H_2O)

CARBON DIOXIDE
(CO_2)

ENERGY
from the sun

GLUCOSE
($C_6H_{12}O_6$)

OXYGEN
(O_2)

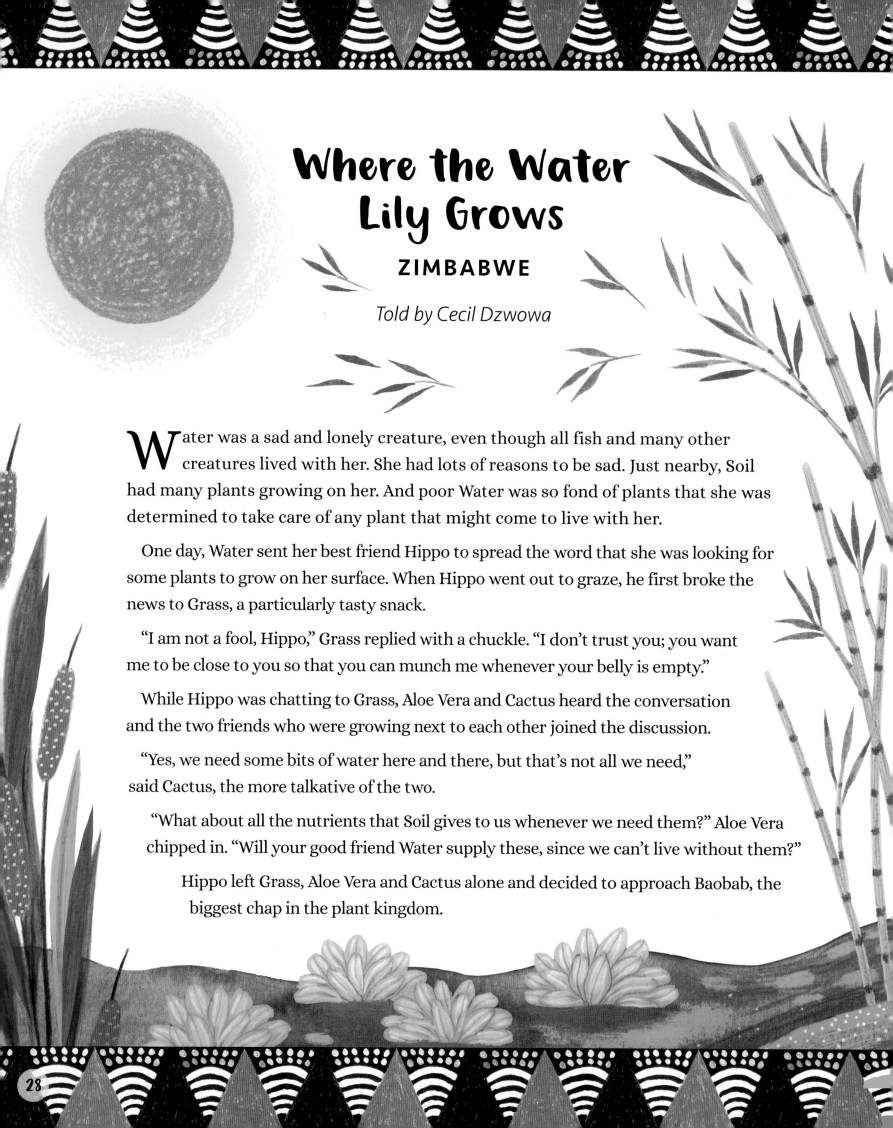

Where the Water Lily Grows

ZIMBABWE

Told by Cecil Dzwowa

Water was a sad and lonely creature, even though all fish and many other creatures lived with her. She had lots of reasons to be sad. Just nearby, Soil had many plants growing on her. And poor Water was so fond of plants that she was determined to take care of any plant that might come to live with her.

One day, Water sent her best friend Hippo to spread the word that she was looking for some plants to grow on her surface. When Hippo went out to graze, he first broke the news to Grass, a particularly tasty snack.

"I am not a fool, Hippo," Grass replied with a chuckle. "I don't trust you; you want me to be close to you so that you can munch me whenever your belly is empty."

While Hippo was chatting to Grass, Aloe Vera and Cactus heard the conversation and the two friends who were growing next to each other joined the discussion.

"Yes, we need some bits of water here and there, but that's not all we need," said Cactus, the more talkative of the two.

"What about all the nutrients that Soil gives to us whenever we need them?" Aloe Vera chipped in. "Will your good friend Water supply these, since we can't live without them?"

Hippo left Grass, Aloe Vera and Cactus alone and decided to approach Baobab, the biggest chap in the plant kingdom.

"I have lived with my friend Soil for hundreds of years. Why should I dump her now?" Baobab asked. "Anyway, your friend Water cannot support my big trunk and roots."

When Hippo returned to Water with the bad news, Water cried bitterly. "Why do these plants dislike me?" she sobbed. "Why, Hippo?"

Hippo felt very sorry for his friend. "Don't worry, I will keep on spreading the word," he said to comfort her. "Maybe one day, some plants will come and stay with you."

Hippo kept his promise. Every time he went out to graze in the jungle, he always encouraged the plants to come and live with Water. However, days, weeks, months and years passed, but the answer Hippo got was the same — a big no.

But when word finally got to Lily, she decided to give it a try. "We are crowded out here on Soil," Lily told Hippo, "and I am ready to move."

When Lily arrived, Water was very excited. At last, a plant was living with her! But Water's luck did not end there. When other plants realized that Lily was now living happily with Water, Reed, Bamboo and a few other plants followed her. Back on the ground with Soil, some plants were making fun of Lily. Some said she was silly, others said she was foolish.

When the wilting plants asked Water if she could help them, she replied, "I have enough plant friends now, but if the drought continues, I will see if a couple more of you can come and join us. And I hope that you will never again forget that Water is every plant and animal's best friend."

Salt WATER

About 97% of Earth's water is ocean — it's **salt water**.

What makes the ocean salty? Rain falls onto land and flows into streams and rivers. **Minerals**, including salt, dissolve from soil and rocks into the flowing water. These are carried into the sea.

More minerals enter the ocean from below. Undersea volcanoes send lava (hot liquid rock from Earth's core) into the water. And jets of boiling hot water spurt from openings deep on the ocean floor, carrying more salts and other minerals.

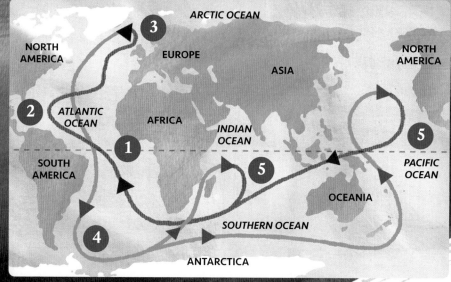

THE GLOBAL CONVEYOR BELT MAP KEY

- - - - - the equator
———— warm water
———— cool water

north / west / east / south

OCEAN IN MOTION

All that salty water isn't just lazing about. Instead, great ribbons of water — ocean currents — constantly move around the seas, forming a **Global Conveyor Belt**. These currents warm and cool Earth.

1 Let's start our round-the-world journey off Africa's west coast. There, at the **equator**, the sun heats the ocean all year long.

2 Winds blowing westwards along the equator create a current — a moving river within the ocean — which flows west and into the Gulf of Mexico. The current of water swirls back around Florida, then turns north and east towards Europe. This warm ocean current is called the Gulf Stream.

3 When winds blow across the Gulf Stream waters, they carry warmth from the water towards the land. Without the Gulf Stream, the weather in Europe would be colder. The water keeps moving northwards, all the way to the Arctic. It gets colder and colder until some freezes into ice. The Gulf Stream ends here, but the water keeps moving along the great Global Conveyor Belt.

4 When ice forms, the salt is squeezed out into the water, making the ocean saltier. And when water gets cold, the molecules move closer together. Cold, salty water is dense. It's heavier than the warmer, less salty water flowing in. So that cold water sinks below the surface, flowing down to the ocean floor. It moves along the bottom, flowing south all the way to Antarctica.

5 The cold water curls back north, some entering the Indian Ocean and some heading into the Pacific Ocean. The moving water mixes with warmer water and begins to rise. Returning to the equator, and warmed again by the sun, the current continues along the surface of the sea. As the water circles, the winds turn it west again, continuing in an endless flow. It takes about a thousand years for a drop of water to complete a full loop around the Global Conveyor Belt.

FANTASTIC PHYTOPLANKTON

Various forms of **PHYTOPLANKTON**, magnified

Ocean currents carry more than heat — they carry oxygen. Fish, like other animals, need oxygen. They don't breathe air but rely on oxygen dissolved in the water. When the water passes over their gills, they absorb the oxygen.

Seawater gets its oxygen from **marine** plants, mostly from **phytoplankton**. Phytoplankton are microscopic — so tiny that you can't see them without a microscope — and you might not have heard of them before. But without them, life in the sea would not survive.

Phytoplankton are types of tiny plants that live in the water. They are usually made of only one cell. Like plants on land, phytoplankton use sunlight and carbon dioxide to make sugar and release oxygen. Some of the oxygen goes into the air and some dissolves in the water.

But phytoplankton need sunlight. They can't live down deep where sun doesn't reach. So how does oxygen get to the creatures living deeper in the ocean? That's where the ocean currents come in! When the water moves from the surface to the ocean floor, the currents bring dissolved oxygen down to the creatures of the deep. This life-giving cycle continues when the currents rise back to the surface. The rising water brings nutrients — things like nitrogen and certain minerals — up from below. The phytoplankton on the surface need these nutrients to live.

Phytoplankton are tiny but mighty!

Phytoplankton are in turn an important food source for the many ocean animals. Others eat the animals that feed on the phytoplankton.

People need phytoplankton too. Why? Oxygen. For millions and billions of years, phytoplankton have been pumping oxygen into the atmosphere — the oxygen the animals on land breathe today. In fact, at least half of the oxygen in the air we breathe is from phytoplankton.

Bursting with Life

Most life on Earth is in the ocean!

From the tiniest phytoplankton to the greatest blue whale, the ocean supports an amazing variety of life. The first living things on Earth appeared in the ocean almost 4 billion years ago.

There are thousands of kinds of **SEAWEED**. Some are fragile and frilly, some float freely on the ocean surface and some fasten themselves to rocks, creating giant forests.

Of course, the ocean supports many **FISH**, from angelfish to zebrafish, halibut to herring, mackerel to mahi-mahi and more.

In the sea and along the shores, you'll find **MARINE MAMMALS**, like walruses and whales, seals and sea otters, narwhals and polar bears.

Ocean animals without backbones are called **INVERTEBRATES**. These include sponges, starfish, squid, scallops, shrimp, crabs, conches and more.

Beautiful and mysterious, **JELLYFISH** trail long tentacles that can sting their prey. Without arms or fins, a jellyfish squeezes its body to move, sending out a squirt of water that pushes it forwards.

Watch out for birds too! From common gulls and ducks to far-off albatrosses and penguins, **SEABIRDS** depend on the ocean for food and more.

Mysteries of the Deep

The ocean holds many wonders, and we're still discovering new ones, like giant tube worms! In 1977, a group of scientists were exploring mysterious hot springs, called hydrothermal vents, deep down on the ocean floor. At these spots, underwater volcanoes heat the water up to an amazing 700°F (371°C). That's even hotter than your oven at home on the highest setting!

At a vent on the ocean floor near the Galapagos Islands, 1.5 miles (2.4 km) below the surface, they discovered creatures no one had ever seen before (see map on pages 10–11). Two years later, a team returned with a deep-sea research vehicle to collect samples of amazing 8-foot-long (2.5 m) giant tube worms. These worms are able to live their entire lives in the deep darkness.

There's still more to explore. Most of the ocean's wonders are yet unseen by human eyes. Mysterious blue holes (underwater sinkholes), deep trenches and undiscovered species await. Who knows what strange and wonderful things are out there?

Sea Changes

The ocean is so vast, you might think nothing could hurt it. But in fact, the ocean is facing some big problems:

- **Mounds of plastic float in the sea:** When we throw out plastic products, packages, bags and bottles, many tons of plastic end up in the ocean. Seabirds and animals can get tangled up in plastic bags. Or they think the plastic looks like food, but when they eat it, they get sick.

- **People have overfished:** Overfishing means we have taken so many fish out of the ocean that certain kinds of fish are disappearing.

- **The ocean is heating up:** As air temperatures rise, the ocean gets warmer too. If water temperatures get too high, many ocean plants and animals die.

- **The ocean is absorbing more carbon dioxide:** Burning fossil fuels (like coal and oil) adds carbon dioxide to the atmosphere. As the ocean absorbs more carbon dioxide from the air, it makes the ocean more acidic. This makes it more difficult for many living things in the ocean, including **coral reefs**, to survive.

It's hard to predict how all these changes will turn out for the ocean, for Earth and for life on Earth. But where people have created problems, people can work to fix them.

DIVE DEEPER!

Can you keep our ocean healthy?

33

The Battle of Baal and Yamm

LEBANON

Retold by Wafa' Tarnowska

Long ago, during the times of the great mariners of Phoenicia, lived the father of all gods, El. He shared his heavenly palace over the mountains of Lebanon with his wife Lady Asherah, the powerful, magnificent mother, and their many children.

Their firstborn was Yamm, the god of the seas and storms. He lived deep in the Mediterranean waters and was worshipped by all sailors to keep them safe during their treacherous voyages.

Their second born was Baal, the god of rain and rider of the clouds. He brought agriculture to the land and lived on Mount Saphon in the north. He was worshipped by farmers and city dwellers alike because he brought order into chaos and kept all floods at bay with his magic thunderbolt.

And then there was Anat, the goddess of war. She loved her brother Baal more than she did Yamm. (These things happen.)

One day, the mighty god El invited his children to a banquet in his great hall and announced that his eldest son, Yamm, would succeed him to the throne. None of Phoenicia's sailors were pleased because Yamm had an unpredictable temper, just like the sea. He could be gentle and calm one day or frightening and fearsome the other. When they heard the news, sailors locked themselves in their homes and refused to sail.

This angered Yamm, who commanded the waves to pound their ports and flood their shores. So the sailors cried to the great Asherah and begged her to intervene.

Lady Asherah went to her son, Yamm. She asked him to calm the waves and release his grip of the winds and storms battering the cities on the coast. Yamm stubbornly refused. Lady Asherah then called on her other son, Baal, to fight his brother, Yamm. She hoped if Baal won that chaos would subside, and peace and order would return to the land.

Riding the clouds, Baal flew to a great craftsman and asked him to make an invincible weapon to defeat Yamm. The craftsman carved two magical clubs of strong and fragrant cedar wood. One club was called Yagrush and the other was called Aymur.

Carrying the magical clubs, Baal summoned Yamm to a duel on Mount Saphon. For days on end, they battled. At times, Yamm transformed himself into a seven-headed serpent while Baal used his thunderbolts to strike at his heads. But Yamm would not be defeated. His joints did not break, and his body did not collapse.

Baal grabbed Yagrush. It swooped from his fingers like an eagle and struck Yamm's shoulders. But Yamm was still not vanquished. So his sister, Anat, handed him Aymur, which she had infused with her mighty energy. Baal held Aymur high and struck Yamm between the eyes. Yamm's joints quivered, his spine shook, and he sank with a thud. He was finally defeated. Baal dragged him down the mountain and dropped him back into the sea. The sea calmed down immediately. Sailors went out to their boats to repair their sails in preparation for their next voyage.

With time, the land grew fertile with the regular rain Baal showered upon it. Delicious fruits grew along its coast: bananas, mandarins, lemons and oranges. Peace and plenty blessed the people as the great Baal — the lord of the rain, the rider of the clouds — was crowned the new king.

Fresh WATER

With all that water in the ocean, just 3% of Earth's water is fresh, not salty.

And of this **fresh water**, most is frozen solid! Two-thirds of Earth's fresh water is ice, in glaciers, ice caps and icebergs. All this ice makes up about 2% of Earth's water. There's also a little bit that drifts through the air as a gas. Just about 1% of Earth's water is fresh AND liquid. This is water you can drink!

WHERE IS FRESH WATER FOUND?

We know fresh water comes from rain. But where does it go? It's not always easy to find. Most fresh water sinks into the ground as groundwater or moisture in the soil. And more bits of water are scattered about in plants and animals — and you.

How much is left as fresh water to fill our lakes, rivers and ponds? About 0.3% of all Earth's water.

DIVE DEEPER!

What can you find in a pond?

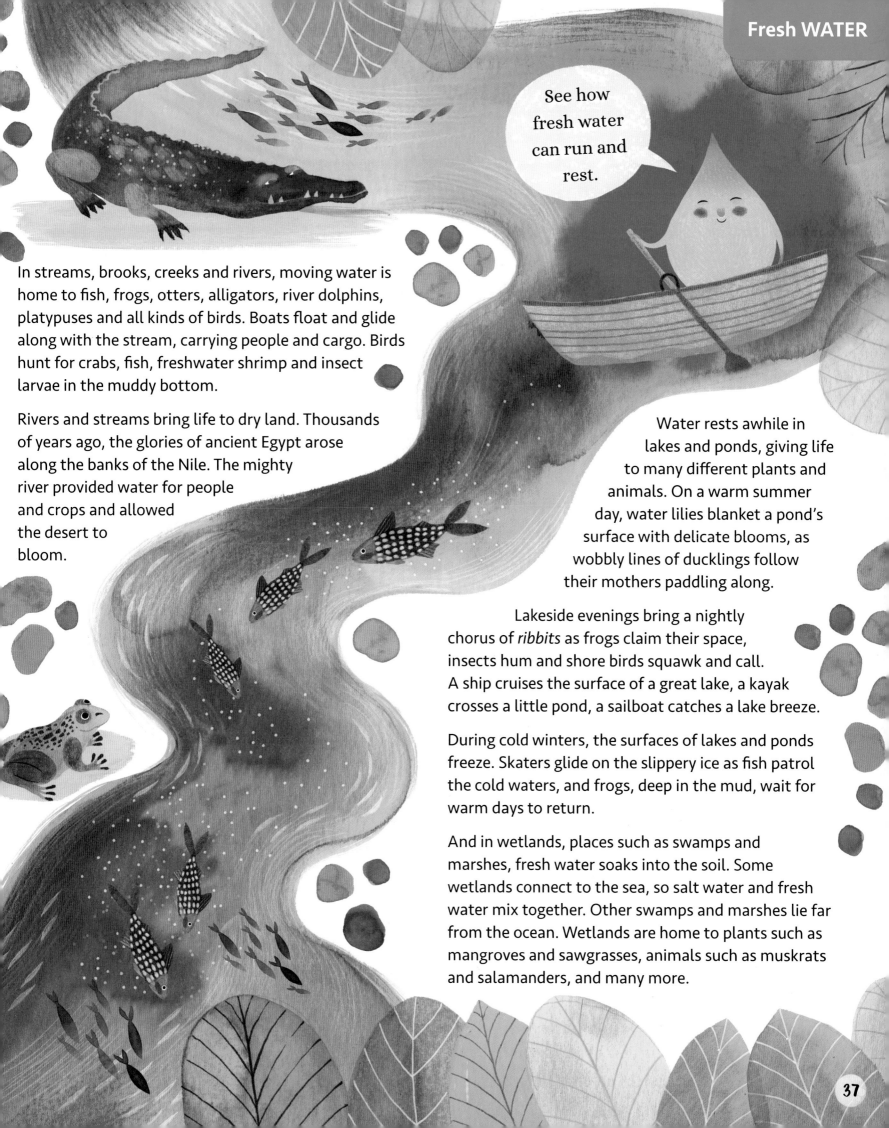

See how fresh water can run and rest.

In streams, brooks, creeks and rivers, moving water is home to fish, frogs, otters, alligators, river dolphins, platypuses and all kinds of birds. Boats float and glide along with the stream, carrying people and cargo. Birds hunt for crabs, fish, freshwater shrimp and insect larvae in the muddy bottom.

Rivers and streams bring life to dry land. Thousands of years ago, the glories of ancient Egypt arose along the banks of the Nile. The mighty river provided water for people and crops and allowed the desert to bloom.

Water rests awhile in lakes and ponds, giving life to many different plants and animals. On a warm summer day, water lilies blanket a pond's surface with delicate blooms, as wobbly lines of ducklings follow their mothers paddling along.

Lakeside evenings bring a nightly chorus of *ribbits* as frogs claim their space, insects hum and shore birds squawk and call. A ship cruises the surface of a great lake, a kayak crosses a little pond, a sailboat catches a lake breeze.

During cold winters, the surfaces of lakes and ponds freeze. Skaters glide on the slippery ice as fish patrol the cold waters, and frogs, deep in the mud, wait for warm days to return.

And in wetlands, places such as swamps and marshes, fresh water soaks into the soil. Some wetlands connect to the sea, so salt water and fresh water mix together. Other swamps and marshes lie far from the ocean. Wetlands are home to plants such as mangroves and sawgrasses, animals such as muskrats and salamanders, and many more.

37

WHERE DOES THE RAIN FALL?

The amount of rain that falls on a place affects all life there.

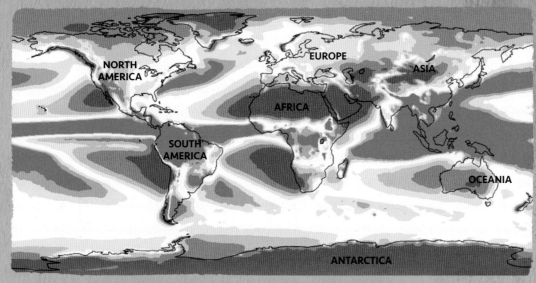

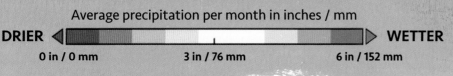

Average precipitation per month in inches / mm

DRIER ◁ ▷ WETTER

0 in / 0 mm   3 in / 76 mm   6 in / 152 mm

Rain does not fall evenly around the world. Let's take a look!

Different amounts of **precipitation** — that's rain, snow, sleet, etc. — fall on different places on Earth. This map shows average amounts of precipitation per month for 1980 to 2020. But scientists say that warmer temperatures are causing rainfall patterns to change over time.

The areas with the least precipitation are deserts. We usually think of deserts as hot, dry places. But Earth's largest desert isn't hot — it's cold, very cold! It's Antarctica. Hardly any snow or rain falls there . . . and when it does, it stays frozen as ice.

Most deserts are hot during the day and get cold at night. The great Sahara (see map on pages 10–11), Earth's largest hot desert, covers most of northern Africa. Parts of the Sahara get no rain at all for years at a time.

Desert plants and animals have unique ways to survive with the tiny amounts of water they can find. A cactus, for example, stores water in its stem.

Certain desert insects find water in the air. The Namib Desert beetle has bumps on its body that make water condense from the air onto the beetle's shell. Special grooves on the shell make the water roll into the beetle's waiting mouth.

Sometimes, the groundwater beneath a desert comes to the surface through a spring. Around such a spot, an **oasis** grows — a green island in the desert. When a camel reaches an oasis after a long, hot walk, it often drinks a huge amount of water — up to 20 gallons (75 L) at once. Camels can store water for long periods — not in their humps, which store fat, but in their blood.

The opposite of deserts are **rainforests**, the wettest places on Earth. The largest rainforest is South America's vast Amazon (see map on pages 10–11). Tropical rainforests are warm, moist jungles that receive between 50 and 260 inches (125–660 cm) of rain per year. That's a lot of rain!

All that water and plenty of sunshine support an astonishing diversity of animals and plants. In fact, though rainforests cover only about 2% of Earth, they are home to about half of the plants and animals on the planet. Every year, scientists find new kinds of living things in the rainforests — and many more remain to be discovered.

In the animal world, sloths and ocelots, macaws and monkeys, capybaras and cassowaries cavort in rainforests. So do more than a thousand kinds of frogs — many of them bright and poisonous — and millions of insect species, from venomous ants to tarantulas the size of dinner plates.

More kinds of trees live in rainforests than any other forests. They're surrounded by glorious flowers and wildly winding vines. Rainforests are so moist, some plants living there don't even need roots to pull water from the soil. Plants such as orchids and ferns grow on the trunks or stems of other plants. They get water from rain and from the air.

TOO MUCH!

Water brings life . . .
but it can also bring destruction.

Floods have happened for millions of years. Waters spill over the banks of rivers or lakes, or hurricanes and other storms send ocean tides high across land that is usually dry.

At times, floods are welcome. The lands around rivers such as the Mississippi, the Nile and the Tigris are very fertile, or especially good for growing crops. This is because floodwaters have left behind a rich layer of **silt** (soil filled with nutrients) as the rivers have overflowed their banks again and again.

Sometimes, farmers flood their fields on purpose during the growing season. Crops such as rice grow best in very wet soil, even in standing water in some cases.

Other times, floods bring disaster. Waters overflow into cities and towns and destroy bridges, roads, houses and entire towns. These losses are painful and rebuilding takes a long time.

Flooding can also spread pollution. If floodwaters damage factories or wastewater treatment plants, the water gets polluted. Chemicals and other waste in the water can spread and make people sick.

Rimac
and Chaclla

PERU

Retold by Mariana Llanos

A long time ago, in the Hanan Pacha, the sky above the Andes mountains, lived a young man called Rimac. His father was Inti, the sun. Rimac loved mingling with humans in this world, the Kay Pacha. His enthralled audience *oohed* and *aahed* at his fascinating stories. Sometimes Rimac's younger sister, Chaclla, came along, although she was extremely shy and wouldn't say a word.

One day, when Rimac and Chaclla came down to visit, they realized the children's eyes had lost their sparkle and their faces frowned. The grown-ups sat around like motionless lumps on the ground. "What happened?" asked Rimac.

"Our crops and animals are dead. We have nothing to eat or drink," said a child.

"It hasn't rained in so long," said a young mother. "I can't remember the sound of rain."

Rimac looked around and saw desolation in their land. The humans had not paid tribute to Mama Pacha, mother earth. They had littered instead; they had forgotten to respect her.

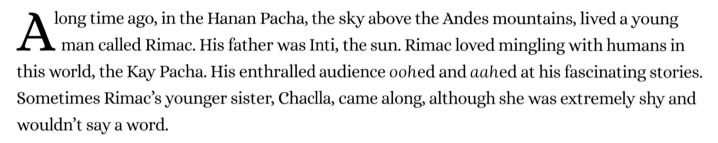

Rimac and Chaclla hurried back to their father, Inti.

"Do something, father!" begged Rimac. "Humans need our help!"

"I can't do anything, son. The humans have brought this upon themselves by not respecting Mama Pacha."

"But I'll teach them to respect her!" cried the young man.
Rimac and Chaclla looked at their father with pleading faces.

Inti sighed heavily. He liked the humans too. He closed his eyes, thinking. "I know a way, but it will only work if one of my children gives up their human form."

Rimac declared, "I'll do it. I'll save them."

"No!" said the sweet but determined voice of Chaclla. She stood by the fire. "They'll miss your stories. I'll do it."

Before Rimac could stop her, Chaclla jumped into the fire and disappeared. Rimac turned to his father. "Humans will have Chaclla and me." Inti nodded because he knew he couldn't stop his strong-willed children. Immediately, Rimac vanished into the fire.

Chaclla and Rimac fell from the Hanan Pacha like ashes from the sky. Once they touched Kay Pacha's mountaintop, they turned into water. First a stream, then a river, they ran happily down the mountain. Humans were excited to see a river rolling down by their homes. They drank its water and refreshed their bodies.

Meanwhile, Chaclla and Rimac kept their frolicking run towards the ocean. Once in the ocean, Chaclla jumped in the air and turned into a cloud. She rained down onto the people over and over. Children and grown-ups danced, laughed and thanked their gods. One day, Chaclla turned into rain forever while Rimac remained a river.

Even today, people hear Rimac's chatter rumbling through the city of Lima. When humans disrespect Mama Pacha, he goes out of his way to warn them. And on days when Chaclla comes to visit, people can hear them laughing.

The Power of WATER

A drop of water seems small, weak, insignificant, easy to ignore . . .

But when many drops of water join together, they are mighty.

Water reshapes the world.

WATER'S SUPERPOWERS

Raindrops dip into dirt, digging little holes in sand or soil. Pouring rain can tear channels in the ground. Fast-moving floodwaters can topple buildings, rip up trees and send walls of mud sliding down hillsides. This is the power of **erosion**!

Other times, erosion works gradually: Bit by bit, a river wears away its banks. Year after year, it cuts a path through soil and stone — deeper and wider, slow and sure. Over millions of years, water can carve a canyon. The Grand Canyon in the United States, Fish River Canyon in Namibia, Tiger Leaping Gorge in China . . . Water made these deep gorges in the earth.

The ocean, too, moves sand and soil and stone. Beaches build, then retreat. Waves crash against cliffs. Blasting rock, the water creates sea caves, airy chambers with rock above and sea below.

The bright Painted Cave of California; the magical Merlin's Cave of England; the glowing Blue Grotto of Italy . . . Water made these.

Water has another important superpower: It fights fires! When firefighters spray water on flames, the water absorbs the heat. You can see the steam as the water turns to gas.

Ice has power too. In a sudden avalanche, a mass of ice, snow and rocks crashes down a mountainside, flattening anything in its path. More often, ice works slowly. Glaciers carve the land. Massive mounds and sheets of ice creep downhill, shoving rocks and sand and gravel ahead. Glaciers grind and scrape, cut and smooth.

During long-ago Ice Ages, vast glaciers covered much of Earth. Over millions of years, the ice cut through cliffs and peaks and dug lakes and ponds: The Finger Lakes of northern New York; the long, narrow fjords of Norway and Greenland; the Matterhorn of Switzerland and Italy... Ice shaped these.

Ice breaks up rocks and roads. Water seeps into a gap in a rock, then freezes into ice. The ice, expanding, splits the rock in two. Water gets into roadway cracks, then freezes and expands, thaws and refreezes, until ruts open up in the surface.

> As ice, water can destroy and create... and send you speeding downhill!

Of course, water's greatest superpower is... bringing life!

1. Picture a dry valley during a long, hot, rainless summer. A small brook dries up, the dry earth around it cracking. Plants wilt and drop their leaves and there are no animals to be seen.

2. Look! Beavers! Watch what happens next. With sticks and small logs, the beavers build a dam, blocking the trickling brook. The water backs up and forms a pool. A pond is born.

3. Over time, fish, turtles, frogs and dragonflies fill the pond with life. Great blue herons hunt. A meadow blooms, then trees grow. All this, because of the water the beavers' dam brought.

HOW WE USE WATER

People harness water's power in many ways.

WE USE WATER TO CREATE FOOD. Farmers grow many plants, from fruit trees to watermelon vines, and crops like corn, wheat, beans and peas. These crops need water. Many farmers must wait and hope for rain to water their fields.

Others are able to **irrigate** their crops, bringing in water through pipes or canals. Farmers have been irrigating for thousands of years, from the times of ancient Egypt, Mesopotamia, Rome and China.

Farmers also raise animals like cows, chickens, pigs and sheep. These animals drink water and they also eat foods that require water to grow.

Do you know how much water was needed to make your dinner?

- To grow the vegetables for a salad with lettuce, tomato and cucumbers takes about 21 gallons (80 L) of water.

- A hamburger (⅓ pound or 150 grams) requires more like 660 gallons (2,500 L). Most of that water is used to grow the grains that feed the cow.

- What about a yummy chocolate bar? To grow the cacao plants and turn the beans into a chocolate bar takes about 450 gallons (1,700 L).

    No water, no chocolate!

WE USE WATER TO KEEP CLEAN.

We use water to flush away our wastes. In much of the world, toilets are filled with clean fresh water. If you think about it, that might seem like a silly way to use precious water, but today's low-flush toilets use less water than old toilets used to. This helps save water for other uses.

Some people are developing ways to take care of our waste without flushing. For example, in a modern composting toilet, human waste (pee and poop) goes into composting bins, where it decomposes into harmless soil with the help of bacteria and natural processes.

We also use water for washing. Water helps us keep things clean: our homes, our clothes, our dishes, ourselves. Soap and water get rid of dirt, oils and germs. That's why washing your hands with soap and water helps stop the spread of bacteria and viruses. It's one of the best ways to stay healthy.

PEOPLE PUT WATER TO WORK IN FACTORIES. Water can help cool machines, and it is also an ingredient in many things produced in factories. Just look how much water it takes to make these familiar things:

- 1 sheet of paper — about 3 gallons (11 L)

- 1 cotton T-shirt — about 660 gallons (2,500 L)

- 1 smart phone — about 3,200 gallons (12,000 L)

- 1 car — between 13,000 and 22,000 gallons (50,000–80,000 L)

Even making this book used water — about 200 gallons (750 L). Can you find something in your home that holds 1 gallon of liquid (such as a milk jug or juice carton)? Now try to imagine what 200 gallons (750 L) would look like!

Quenching the World's Thirst

All around the world, people quench their thirst with cool, sweet water.

For many, it's easy — just turn the tap and clean fresh water pours out. It arrives through pipes, flowing from a local river, or from melted snow that fell on far-off mountains, or from groundwater pumped from underground, or from rainfall stored in a town reservoir. There's plenty of water to drink, wash and even play with!

For other people, getting enough water requires more effort. You might collect it from melting glaciers, or pull up a bucketful at a town well, or push the handle of a village pump, or dip into a central spring shared by local residents.

And in some places, getting a drink of water is really quite difficult. About 785 million people around the world — one out of ten — have no running water in their homes or even nearby. They may live in an area that gets very little rain. Maybe their traditional water supply has dried up or their community doesn't have water pumps and pipes.

If you live in such a place, you must travel a long way to fetch water. You walk on rough paths to a far-off stream or spring, carrying a large jar or urn. You scoop the water up, fill your jar and carry the heavy water on the long walk back home to your family. You do this every day, perhaps twice a day.

People around the world are finding new ways to collect clean water.

In Middle Eastern deserts, farmers have built **greenhouses** to grow crops using salt water. Inside the greenhouse, the water is evaporated. It condenses as fresh water, which is good for the plants.

In some places near the ocean, people drink seawater — but first, they remove the salt and other minerals, a process called desalination. Running large desalination plants is expensive and uses a great deal of energy. That's why desalination has been used mainly in the Middle East and North Africa, very dry places with resources to operate these plants.

Governments, organizations and volunteers know that everyone should have clean drinking water close to home, so many people are working to make that happen. Together, they're drilling wells to bring fresh water up from underground. They're laying pipes to carry water into villages. They're replacing old water sources with new ones.

Who are the people doing this?

GEORGIE BADIEL is one.

Georgie grew up in a village in Burkina Faso, in West Africa (see map on pages 10–11). As a girl, she spent three hours each day walking from her home to a water hole and carrying water back. Fetching water is a job almost always given to girls and women. Georgie scooped water into a big jug and carried it home. Then she turned around to make another trip for another heavy jug of water.

She grew up and worked hard to become a successful fashion model. She even won the Miss Africa title in 2004. Then she used her success to start an organization, the Georgie Badiel Foundation, to help villages in her country drill wells. When villages have clean well water, their girls can go to school instead of carrying water all day long. In places like Georgie's village, running water means more girls in school.

The Mystery of the Watering Hole

SAINT LUCIA

Retold by Baptiste Paul

One misty night, villagers gathered to mourn Mr. Lewis — the best storyteller they had ever known. They loved hearing tales and thought there was no better way to send Mr. Lewis on his afterlife journey than to share stories in his memory. Brothers Jean and Ti-Jean hurried, but their energy dwindled after hauling water all day. For as long as they could remember, their before and after school tasks were fetching water from the river a few miles away. The boys tucked in around the calabash tree, where the new storyteller stood among a circle of villagers.

"Once, an elder told me there is a watering hole in this very village," the storyteller began. "But a creature named Bolom has been concealing it with magic for centuries." Everyone gasped. "But if anyone finds it, the spell would be broken."

Ti-Jean elbowed Jean. "If we could find that watering hole, we could save a lot of time."

Jean nodded. "Imagine how much football we could play!" Ti-Jean giggled and fist-bumped his brother.

The storyteller's face tightened. "It's no laughing matter, boys. Mark my words, one day you will face the creature."

That night, the boys lay in bed with a prickle of excitement mixed with a pang of dread. Bolom scared them, but what good were adventures without a little risk?

They jumped out of bed and drew a map based on the storyteller's details. They planned their search for the next full moon — when Bolom would reveal itself.

When the time came, the boys slipped past their dad and hiked to an area called Flat Rocks, where their friends believed evil spirits resided. Hovering above the ground, a shadowy figure circled. The boys ducked into the bushes and turned their eyes away to stay safe from the creature's gaze. They thought of turning back, but it was too late. The creature stopped — it knew they were near.

A crackly voice barked. "Come out!" Jean and Ti-Jean inched forwards. Their pelex — the hairs on their necks — stiffened.

Ti-Jean reached for the courage to speak. "We heard about a watering hole. W-w-would you help us find it?"

The shadow grew ten times in size and its voice roared, "NO! LEAVE THIS PLACE."

Jean dropped the map. Ti-Jean threw the buckets towards the shadow. They bolted and found themselves on an unfamiliar path. Panic and confusion set in. They panted for several minutes, trying to stay out of sight. Then the brothers saw golden beams of light glistening on a flat surface.

"Is that . . . water?" whispered Jean.

"I think so!" said Ti-Jean. "Let's leave a trail."

The boys contained their excitement as they cautiously trekked home, marking tree trunks along the way. Soon, they found the path that led to their front door. As Jean turned to grab the doorknob, one slender hand grabbed each of the boys' shoulders and squeezed. They shrieked and turned to see . . .

"Dad?"

"What are you boys doing out so late?" Dad scolded. "It's a full moon. Wouldn't want Bolom to catch you." The boys let out a breath, then darted towards their room.

The next day, in the safety of sunshine, they would gather everyone around the calabash tree and recount their adventure. Then, Jean and Ti-Jean would lead their friends on a short walk to the most glorious watering hole.

WATER Everywhere?

Even though our planet is so watery, in some places there's still not enough water. And some of our water is polluted — full of dirt, chemicals and harmful bacteria. But people can help!

SAVING WATER

There are more and more people living on Earth. People are using more and more water for farms, factories, flushing and all sorts of other things. However, the amount of water on Earth has remained the same for about four billion years. That's all we've got. That's why many people are thinking about ways to save water.

Here are some smart ideas that people are trying:

- **CLEANING UP WASTEWATER** so we can use it again after we flush it down the toilet. Cleaned-up wastewater can be used to water plants, flush more toilets or keep factories running. In fact, in some places, this water is cleaned so well that it's good enough to drink.

- **MAKING "DRIER" CLOTHES!** Your jeans might not feel wet, but a lot of water went into making them. Companies are inventing new ways to manufacture clothing with less water. They are also using recycled materials like old cotton clothes and even plastic water bottles. All this can save millions of gallons of water.

- **USING REUSABLE WATER BOTTLES:** If you can, avoid disposable plastic water bottles. Plastic bottles require more water to make than they can hold — three times more. In many places, you can pour water from your tap into a reusable bottle instead.

DIVE DEEPER!

How can you help save water?

KEEPING IT CLEAN

Sometimes, pollution gets into our water from factories, oil spills or human waste. If our water gets dirty, we can work together to clean it up so our waters can run clear and clean again.

Pollution is bad for animals, plants and people.

For many years, New York's Hudson River was so full of stinky chemicals that fish couldn't live in it. In the 1960s, people got together to save their river. They stopped factories from dumping chemicals into it and started cleaning those chemicals out of the river. Today, people can swim in the Hudson. And the fish — and other living things that depend on the river — are much happier!

Solving problems like this takes lots of money and often years of hard work.

AUTUMN PELTIER started speaking out about clean water as a young girl. She is a member of the Wikwemikong First Nation, an Indigenous community of Ontario, Canada (see map on pages 10–11). When she was eight years old, she visited a First Nation community where the residents had to boil their water before they could drink it. She was shocked. This inspired her to become an activist.

Autumn believes that everyone has the right to clean water. She met with the Canadian Prime Minister, saying she was disappointed that the government had approved oil pipelines that caused water pollution in First Nation communities. He promised to protect the water, and since then the Canadian government has cleaned up polluted water in many communities.

Autumn fights for clean water for Indigenous communities in Canada and for people around the world. As a teenager, she gave several speeches about the importance of clean water at the United Nations. At age 14, she was named the chief water commissioner of the Anishinabek Nation, an advocacy organization for First Nations groups.

Autumn has said, "I advocate for water because we all came from water and water is literally the only reason we are here today and living on this earth." And because water does not speak for itself, Autumn says, "I speak for the water."

Together, let's **RESPECT** and **PROTECT** Earth's water — our water —
THE ONLY WATER WE HAVE.

Water in the World of Work

Do you like to play with water? Maybe someday you'll find a job working with water. From firefighters to ski instructors to oceanographers, many people use water in their work. Their jobs may take them into, onto or around water every day.

Here are some watery ways to work — can you think of others?

Would you like to work with water when you grow up?

NGINEER
ges, sewers
r systems

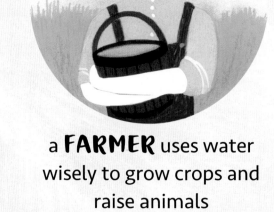

a **FARMER** uses water wisely to grow crops and raise animals

G BOAT
N brings
o market

a **HYDROLOGIST** studies the science of water and its flow

EGUARD
immers safe
e water

a **MARINE BIOLOGIST** studies the plants and animals of the ocean

a **METEOROLOGIST**
studies and forecasts
the weather

an **OCEANOGRAPHER**
studies ocean currents or
chemicals in seawater

a **PEARL DIVER**
dives down into salty seas
in search of oysters

a **RAFTING GUIDE**
leads river adventures
down rushing rapids

a **SAILOR** helps to
sail a big ship across
lakes and seas

a **SKI INSTRUCTOR**
zips down a snowy
mountainside

a **WATER ACTIVIST**
works to keep water
clean and safe for all

a **WATER QUALITY
ANALYST** tests
how clean our water is

a **WELL DRILLER**
digs wells to bring water
up from underground

53

The River Sisters

CHINA

Told by Xinran

A long, long time ago, on the Tibetan Plateau, the world's highest and largest plateau, lived two sisters: the Yellow River and the Yangzi River. They often heard the Queen Mother of Heaven say that China in the east was very vast and magical, so the sisters decided to go down to explore the mysteries of China.

Sister Yellow River had a cheerful and straightforward personality, and she liked to go on adventures. She'd heard that northern China was much colder and full of mountains, where human nature was bold — even the food there was spicy hot. So she decided to go to northern China.

Sister Yangzi River's personality was very different from her sister Yellow River. Quite introverted, she liked flowers and plants. She'd heard that the climate of southern China was warm and wet, where people were elegant and delicate and their food was sweet and mild. So she wanted to go to southern China.

Big sister Yellow River set out from the north and soon met her lover Tibetan Plateau, so they got married there. They enjoyed their grazing migration between the seasons. Their grandchildren continued their grandmother's wish to go on exploring, many of them settling by the mountains along the Yellow River and helping northern people cultivate wheat, corn and cotton. Year after year, the descendants of the Yellow River have created China's three thousand years of Yellow River civilization.

Younger sister Yangzi River set out from the south and soon met and fell in love with the Hengduan Mountains. The Hengduan Mountains hugged their beloved Yangzi River and together visited Yunnan, Sichuan Province. Over fifty ethnic minority groups living along the river received their love and support over the years. Finally, they came to a large green plain, where they decided to settle down and raise children together. Their descendants continued to travel east and follow the dream of their grandmother. Many of them settled in the gentle hills of southern China, growing rice, feeding fish and shrimp, and making the south become the richest area in all of China. The descendants of the Yangzi River have given birth to the Yangzi River civilization with fish, rice, flowers all year round and hundreds of thousands of poems.

The children of the Yellow River and the Yangzi River are reunited in the Pacific Ocean every year. There, they also see some new friends from the seven continents and the five oceans. At that time, some of them will turn into tiny angels made of mist, heading up into the sky to see the ancestors of the Queen Mother, while also taking with them the family blessings from the Yellow River, the Yangzi River and China.

What Does the Future Hold for Earth's Water?

Whether you live in a desert or a rainforest
or somewhere in between,
you are part of the water cycle.
Water brings life to you and your family,
to the plants and animals around you.

As water cycles around the world,
across the land, from mountains to rivers,
into the air and through the clouds,
in and out of our bodies, around
huge whales and tiny plankton,
slippery eels, graceful rays
and radiant schools of fish,
it supports life everywhere.
Water renews Earth.

Thanks for exploring the world of water with me. Remember — water is life!

A drop of water that a dinosaur drank 66 million years ago,
that flowed down the Nile in ancient Egypt,
that helped put out a forest fire twenty years ago,
that ran through your water pipes and into your glass today,
is one small part of an endless cycle.

That water is a treasure.
It belongs to Earth
and is part of us all.

atom: the most basic building block of all matter, so small that you cannot see it even with a regular microscope

carbon dioxide: a gas that is a mixture of carbon and oxygen

climate: the usual weather conditions in a place over a long period of time

condensation: the changing of matter from gas form into liquid form

coral reef: a warm-water ocean environment made up of coral skeletons, where many plants and animals live

deposition: the changing of matter from gas form directly to solid form without passing through a liquid phase

desert: a dry area of Earth that receives very little precipitation

element: a type of matter made of a single type of atom, such as oxygen or gold

equator: an imaginary circle around the middle of Earth, halfway between the North and South Poles

erosion: the wearing away of land or rock by water, ice or wind

evaporation: the changing of matter from liquid form to gas form

filter: something that removes dirt from a liquid or gas that passes through it

fresh water: water that is not salty

gas: a form of matter, like air, that has no shape and spreads out to fill whatever space it is in

glacier: a massive, slow-moving chunk of ice in high mountains or near Earth's poles

Global Conveyor Belt: the system of ocean currents carrying water from the ocean bottom to the surface and around the globe

greenhouse: a building for growing plants indoors, with controlled lighting, heat and water

groundwater: water that lies underground in the soil and the cracks of rock layers

irrigate: to bring water to crops through pipes, canals or other man-made means

lagoon: an area of shallow salt water separated from the ocean by a coral reef or sand bank

mammal: an animal that is warm-blooded and whose young drink milk from their mother

marine: relating to the ocean

matter: something that has weight and takes up space, which can be in solid, liquid or gas form

microscopic: so small that you need a microscope to see it

minerals: solid materials present in nature that do not come from plants or animals

molecule: a group of atoms bonded together

nutrients: things that plants and animals need to stay strong and healthy, such as protein, minerals and vitamins

oasis: a spot in a desert where water comes up to the surface from underground, allowing trees and other plants to grow

oxygen: a gas found in Earth's air and water, which animals need to breathe

photosynthesis: the process by which plants use sunlight to turn water and carbon dioxide into sugar, producing oxygen as well

phytoplankton: microscopic green plants that live in the upper layers of the ocean

pollution: harmful chemicals, waste or exhaust that make the air, water or soil dirty and unhealthy for living things

precipitation: water falling from the sky, as rain, sleet, hail or snow

rainforest: a warm, moist, wooded area with very high rainfall, where many different kinds of plants and animals live

salt water: water containing high amounts of dissolved salts, such as in the ocean

silt: small bits of soil and rock that are carried by flowing water and settle to the bottom of still water

sublimation: the changing of matter from solid form directly to gas form without passing through a liquid phase

transpiration: the process by which plants release water (in gas form) into the air

water cycle: water's movement as it evaporates into the air, falls as precipitation, collects on the planet's surface and continues around Earth

water vapor/vapour: the gas form of water

weather: the condition of the air outside, such as hot, cold, wet, dry, calm, windy, clear or cloudy

wetlands: areas of land where the soil contains a great deal of water

zooplankton: drifting water creatures, usually microscopic, but also including jellyfish and the young life stages of other larger animals

Behind the Stories

More than just water went into making this book!

A Note from the Publisher

This book introduces readers to the beauty, power and importance of water — not only through facts and information, but also through eight stories from different cultures and countries. On the following pages, you can find out more about the people who wrote and illustrated this book. They come from all over the world! Can you find where each person lives on a map or globe?

We invite readers to continue their exploration of water in the future. What types of stories could you tell about water and how it plays a role in your life? What areas of water have you visited? Where would you like to travel to see more amazing water? How can you help take care of our natural resources and precious world?

For more information visit www.barefootbooks.com/water

Sources and Credits

A great deal of research went into this book. Among other sources, we consulted a range of academic and government authorities, including NOAA, NASA, USGS, EPA, NIH, Smithsonian Museum and the United Nations. When we found different sources provided differing facts or figures, we relied on those given by National Geographic publications.

Credit for map on p38:
Global precipitation climatology map courtesy of Salient Predictions (2020)

Units of Measurement

We can measure the world around us in all kinds of ways — distance, volume, temperature, weight and more. Different units are used to describe different types of measurements. There are two main systems of measurement units. The customary system in the United States uses units such as gallons and miles. The metric system, used in science and in most countries, has units such as liters / litres (L) and kilometers / kilometres (km). This book gives measurements in both systems, with customary units first followed by metric equivalents.

Christy Mihaly

has written more than 25 children's books, mostly nonfiction. She has degrees in policy studies, environmental studies and law from Dartmouth College and the University of California, Berkeley. She lives with her family in Vermont, where she enjoys the inspiration of the changing seasons and the endless varieties of New England precipitation.

She has paddled a canoe down remote river rapids, examined drops of pond water under a microscope, waded through babbling brooks in search of dragonfly larvae and helped protect wild waterfalls in her home state of Vermont. You could say she has water in her blood (don't we all?). Christy finds water endlessly fascinating, and she hopes that you will too!

"It has been a thrill to put this beautiful book together with the brilliant team at Barefoot Books. My goal was to spark in readers a sense of the wonder and miracle of water. With a deep understanding of how water works and how it sustains life on our planet, we can cherish and protect it." — Christy Mihaly

"I have really enjoyed creating the illustrations for this book; water is such a necessary, vital, powerful and versatile element. It is so integral to our lives that it is easy to take it for granted. Watching, listening to and attending it as I have for this work has led me to a deep appreciation and vision which I hope to have shared with my brushes and pencils." — Mariona Cabassa

Mariona Cabassa

is a native of Catalunya who has illustrated over 80 children's books. She studied at art school in Barcelona, Spain, followed by further research in Strasbourg, France. Her many subsequent years of working as an illustrator, painter, installation maker and tattoo artist reflect her fascination with form and her desire to explore different palettes. Mariona's technique combines water-based paints, pencils and a digital touch to create rich and detailed illustrations, bursting with life and movement.

Thank you!

Barefoot Books is indebted to many people for their help in the creation of this book, especially:

Nancy Copley, marine biologist, and **Ray Schmitt**, physical oceanographer, both of the Woods Hole Oceanographic Institution (Falmouth, MA, USA)

María-Verónica A. Barnes, Director of Diversity Education at Lexington Montessori School (Lexington, MA, USA)

Tekelmarae and the Boy Who Remembered —
VANUATU (pages 8–9)

Selina Tusitala Marsh was born in
Aotearoa, New Zealand.
Her mum comes from
Samoa and Tuvalu
and her dad is a New
Zealander. Tusitala
means storyteller.
That's what she does
as an Associate Professor at
Auckland University and as a Poet.

Te Auaunga Waterfall, Auckland, NZ

Pala Molisa is from Vanlav and Ambae in Vanuatu
and has lived in New Zealand since he was 13 years old.
Pala is a lecturer in Business and Leadership studies and an
Emotional Anatomy therapist. He teaches about the stories
our bodies tell us. This story was inspired by tales told by
Pala's dad, Sela Molisa, and his grandad, Pupui Mandei.

The River of Life — INDIA (pages 12–13)

Meera Sriram has lived almost equal parts
of her life in India and the US. She is the author of
several picture books including *A Gift for Amma* and
Dumpling Day, and has also co-authored kids' books
in India. Meera believes in the power of stories and
likes to write about people and places less visible in
children's literature.

For this project, Meera was
inspired to celebrate
rivers as the lifeblood
of our planet. She was
particularly drawn to
retell a story about
Kaveri, a river steeped in
myths and legends that
feeds the soul of southern
India where she grew up.

The Waters of Sulis — ENGLAND (pages 20–21)

Xanthe Gresham Knight
grew up bumping into trees and lampposts
while memorizing stories and was knocked out
by the tale of Sulis from Bath.

Now an acclaimed writer and international
storyteller, who the British Theatre Review described
as "unfolding each story like the petals of a lotus,"
Xanthe is delighted to
offer her version of
this English myth.
She is the author
of many books for
children, including
*Thumbelina, Wild
Swans* and *The
Snow Queen.*

Photograph by Mishko Papic

Where the Water Lily Grows — ZIMBABWE (pages 28–29)

Cecil Dzwowa was born in Chiredzi in southern
Zimbabwe in 1970. He trained as a primary school
teacher at Seke Teachers' College with English as his main
subject of study. Using this English teaching background
as a launchpad, in 1999 he became a freelance writer
specializing in children's magazines. As a writer, some of
his articles were published in USA-based magazines like
Highlights for Children, Faces and *Odyssey*.

Cecil believes that water
is one of the most
important components
of life on our planet.
"Where the Water
Lily Grows" was
an opportunity to
highlight this to
children in a funny but
informative way.

The Battle of Baal and Yamm — LEBANON (pages 34–35)

Wafa' Tarnowska

is an award-winning writer, translator and storyteller. She sees herself as a cultural bridge between East and West and feels particularly proud of her many books for children, including *The Arabian Nights* and *Amazing Women of the Middle East*. She has called many countries her home but currently lives between England and Poland.

Wafa' was born in Lebanon and has always been inspired by the myths of her ancestors, the Phoenicians. Civilization needs water to prosper, so when Baal, the rain god, wins the battle over Yamm, the sea god, rain blessed the earth allowing people to grow crops and have plenty to eat.

Rimac and Chaclla — PERU (pages 40–41)

Mariana Llanos is a

Peruvian-born children's writer who lives in Oklahoma, USA. She is the author of *Run, Little Chaski!* and *Eunice and Kate*, among others.

For this retelling, Mariana found inspiration in a legend compiled by a Peruvian author named Oscar Colchado Lucio. She remembers hearing this story when she was a young student in Peru. Mariana used to live by the shore of the Rimac River in Lima, and she can still remember its captivating chatter.

The Mystery of the Watering Hole — SAINT LUCIA (pages 48–49)

Baptiste Paul

grew up in Saint Lucia, where at age seven he propagated a root cutting that still produces breadfruit for his community. He holds an Environmental Science degree and is the author of several books including *The Field* and *To Carnival! A Celebration in Saint Lucia* as well as co-author of *I Am Farmer*, *Adventures to School* and *Peace* with Miranda Paul. www.BaptistePaul.com

In Saint Lucia, oral storytelling is an important part of the culture. As a child, Baptiste was always fascinated and captivated by Bolom stories told by Ms. Drina Charlery. Unfortunately, she passed away in 2020. She was the best storyteller he ever knew.

The River Sisters — CHINA (pages 54–55)

Xinran

was born in Beijing and moved to London in 1997. Not only a successful journalist and radio presenter, she is also the author of eight nonfiction books. Her first book, *The Good Women of China*, was an international bestseller. In 2004, Xinran set up The Mothers' Bridge of Love, a charity creating a bridge of understanding between China and the West. www.mothersbridge.org

Xinran was brought up on so many imaginative and wonderful Chinese fairy tales, rich arts and ancient poems. As the mothers of 3,000 years of Chinese civilization, the Yellow River and the Yangzi River flow through all of them, just as they do in "The River Sisters."

To Vincent Rae, who is more than 70% water, and to his wonderful, worthy (though less watery) parents.

With deep thanks to the tireless team at Barefoot Books — C. M.

Hope to see you again soon!

To my son, Martin, and to Lupe — both as dear to me as the natural resources of this beautiful planet are.

The careful stewardship of Mother Earth lies in their hands and those of all the coming generations. May they carry that responsibility with grace. It is not too late — M. C.

Barefoot Books
23 Bradford Street, 2nd Floor
Concord, MA 01742

Barefoot Books
29/30 Fitzroy Square
London, W1T 6LQ

Text copyright © 2021 by Christy Mihaly
Illustrations copyright © 2021 by Mariona Cabassa
The moral rights of Christy Mihaly and
Mariona Cabassa have been asserted

"Tekelmarae and the Boy Who Remembered" text copyright
© 2021 by Selina Tusitala Marsh and Pala Molisa
"The River of Life" text copyright © 2021 by Meera Sriram
"The Waters of Sulis" text copyright © 2021 by Xanthe Gresham Knight
"Where the Water Lily Grows" text copyright © 2021 by Cecil Dzwowa
"The Battle of Baal and Yamm" text copyright © 2021 by Wafa' Tarnowska
"Rimac and Chaclla" text copyright © 2021 by Mariana Llanos
"The Mystery of the Watering Hole" text copyright © 2021 by Baptiste Paul
"The River Sisters" text copyright © 2021 by Xinran

First published in the United States of America by Barefoot Books, Inc
and in Great Britain by Barefoot Books, Ltd in 2021
All rights reserved

Graphic design by Sarah Soldano, Barefoot Books
Edited and art directed by Emma Parkin, Barefoot Books
Reproduction by Bright Arts, Hong Kong
Printed in China on 100% acid-free paper
This book was typeset in Alice, Popsicle and Seravek
The illustrations for this book were prepared in pencils,
pastels, water-based paints and a digital touch

ISBN 978-1-64686-280-1 | E-book ISBN 978-1-64686-344-0

British Cataloguing-in-Publication Data: a catalogue record
for this book is available from the British Library

Library of Congress Cataloging-in-Publication Data
is available under LCCN 2021015465

1 3 5 7 9 8 6 4 2